The Official <u>MBA</u> Handbook of Great Business Quotations

Selected by Jim Fisk and Robert Barron

A Fireside Book
Published by Simon & Schuster, Inc.
New York

Contents

It is a good thing for an uneducated man to read books of quotations.

—Winston Churchill

1
Success and Failure

Nothing succeeds like success.

—Alexandre Dumas

Nothing succeeds like excess.

—Oscar Wilde

Nothing recedes like success.

—Walter Winchell

Nothing succeeds like one's own successor.

—Anonymous

If A equals success, then the formula is A = X + Y + Z. X is work, Y is play, Z is keep your mouth shut.

—Albert Einstein

The moral flabbiness born of the bitch-goddess success: that—with the squalid cash interpretation put on the word success—is our national disease.

—William James, professor of psychology, Harvard University

I don't know anything about luck. I've never banked on it, and I'm afraid of people who do. Luck to me is something else: hard work and realizing what is opportunity and what isn't.

—Lucille Ball

There is a master key to success with which no man can fail. Its name is simplicity.

—Henri Detering, former president of Shell Oil, whose master key to success (the simple idea of fixing oil prices with Exxon, Mobil, Gulf, Texaco, SoCal, and British Petroleum) controlled the industry fifty years before OPEC

All you need in this life is ignorance and confidence, and then success is sure.

—Mark Twain

I cannot give you a formula for success, but I can give you the formula for failure: try to please everybody.

—Herbert Bayard Swope

The two leading recipes for success are building a better mousetrap and finding a bigger loophole.

—Edgar A. Schoaff

Success and failure are both difficult to endure. Along with success come drugs, divorce, fornication, bullying, travel, meditation, medication, depression, neurosis and suicide. With failure comes failure.

> —Joseph Heller, author of *Catch 22*

Nice guys finish last.

> —Leo Durocher

Contrary to the cliché, genuinely nice guys most often finish first, or very near it.

> —Malcolm Forbes

Success often comes from taking a misstep in the right direction.

> —Anonymous

The fastest way to succeed is to look as if you're playing by other people's rules, while quietly playing by your own.
—Michael Korda, editor-in-chief of Simon and Schuster and the author of *Success*

It takes twenty years to make an overnight success.

—Eddie Cantor

Success isn't everything, but it makes a man stand straight.

—Lillian Hellman

Success is that old ABC—ability, breaks and courage.

—Charles Luckman

Success is simply a matter of luck. Ask any failure.

—Earl Wilson

If you hype something and succeed, you're a genius—it wasn't hype. If you hype it and it fails, then it's just hype.
—Neil Bogart, president of Casablanca Records,
whose first success was hyping the song
"Yummy, Yummy, Yummy, I've Got Love in My
Tummy," but who was the genius behind artists
like Donna Summer

Success is not so much what you are but rather what you appear to be. Appearance is reality.

—Anonymous

The worst part of having success is to try finding someone who is happy for you.

—Bette Midler

A celebrity is a person who works hard all his life to become known, then wears dark glasses to avoid being recognized.

—Fred Allen

Success is something to enjoy—to flaunt! Otherwise, why work so hard to get it?

—From *Funny Girl*

A lot of executives keep up the pretense of being solid community members when they're sleeping with their secretaries. Hef's honest. He isn't burdened with success.

—Christie Hefner, president of Playboy
Enterprises

Financial success is never having to balance your checkbook.

—Benjamin Graham, dean of American
securities analysts

If at first you don't succeed, you are running about average.

—M. H. Anderson

The classic formula for success is "Dress British, think Yiddish."

—Jim Fisk and Robert Barron

The secret of success in life is for a man to be ready for his opportunity when it comes.

—Benjamin Disraeli, first Jewish prime minister of Britain

2
Power

Power is the ultimate aphrodisiac.
—Henry Kissinger

Charlatanism is to some degree indispensable to effective leadership.
—Eric Hoffer, dockside philosopher

To make an omelet, you have to be willing to break a few eggs.

—Robert Penn Warren

Being powerful is like being a lady. If you have to tell people you are, you aren't.

—Attributed to Margaret Thatcher

If you're rich and famous you don't have any trouble getting laid.

—Marlon Brando

Influence is like a savings account. The less you use it, the more you've got it.

—Andrew Young

I would rather be first in a small village in Gaul than second in command in Rome.

—Julius Caesar

Nearly all men can stand adversity, but if you want to test a man's character, give him power.

—Abraham Lincoln

Power corrupts. Absolute power corrupts absolutely.

—Lord Acton

Security is a smile from a headwaiter.

—Russell Baker

The buck stops here.

—Harry S. Truman

3
The Devil's Bargain

All work and no play makes Jack a dull boy.
—Anonymous

All work and no play makes Jack a dull boy—and
Jill a wealthy widow.
—Evan Esar

All work and no play makes jack.

—Anonymous

The trouble with the rat race is that even if you win, you're still a rat.

—Lily Tomlin

It is easier for a camel to get through the eye of a needle than for a rich man to enter the kingdom of God.

—St. Matthew, XIX, 24

It feels uncommonly queer to have enough cash to pay one's bills. I'd have sold my soul for it a few years ago.

—Edith Wharton

Idealism increases in direct proportion to one's distance from the problem.

—John Galsworthy

Those whom the gods wish to destroy they first call promising.

—Cyril Connolly, British critic

The fast track in business: B.A., M.B.A., C.E.O., . . . D.O.A.

—Jim Fisk and Robert Barron

While I had a regular job, I was too busy to make money.

—A Wall Street financier

4

Office Politics

To get along, go along.
> —Advice given to Lyndon Johnson by his
> mentor, Sam Rayburn

Go with the flow.

> —Ken Kesey

Never learn to do anything. If you don't learn,
you'll always find someone else to do it for you.

—Mark Twain

All animals are equal, but some animals are more
equal than others.

—George Orwell

In the average office, S.O.B. stands for "Son of
Boss."

—Spencer Purinton

What really flatters a man is that you think him
worth flattering.

—George Bernard Shaw

Management is the art of getting other people to do all the work.

—Anonymous

Seeing ourselves as others see us would probably confirm our worst suspicions about them.

—Franklin P. Jones

Deadwood: anyone in your office who is more senior than you are.

—Jim Fisk and Robert Barron

It's not what you say or do that counts but what your posture is when you say or do it.

—Robert Ringer, author of *Winning Through Intimidation*

If you don't say anything, you won't be called upon to repeat it.

    —"Silent Cal" (Calvin Coolidge)

It isn't what you know that counts, it's what you think of in time.

    —Anonymous

You've got to have a personal life and a business life, and keep them as separate as you can. If you don't, you end up sacrificing all the things which were on your mind when you set out down the road to achieve your job.

 —Samuel Armacost, C.E.O. of Bank of America

Originality is the art of remembering what you hear but forgetting where you heard it.

    —Not sure where we heard this one

It is true that we are very close friends, and she's a very close friend of the family. But that has nothing to do with the way I and others in the company evaluate performance.

—William Agee, C.E.O. of Bendix, speaking of Mary Cunningham, V.P. of Strategic Planning for Bendix, who was later to become Mary Cunningham Agee

5
Marketing

Marketing is simply sales with a college education.

—John Freund

Necessity is the mother of invention.

—Plato

Invention is the mother of necessity.
—Thorsten Veblen, social economist and author
of *The Theory of the Leisure Class*

That's where God intended it to be.
—A Ford Motor Company executive,
commenting on the company's decision to move
the horn back from the turn signal lever to the
center of the wheel

You have to do a little bragging on yourself, even
to your relatives. Men just don't get anywhere
without advertising.
—John Nance Garner, former vice president of
the U. S.

Ready, fire, aim!
—Anonymous

Doing business without advertising is like winking at a girl in the dark. *You* know what you're doing, but nobody else does.

—Stewart Henderson Britt

Advertising is the greatest art form of the twentieth century.

—Marshall McLuhan

You may fool all the people some of the time; you can even fool some of the people all the time; but you can't fool all of the people all the time.

—Abraham Lincoln

6
Negotiating

Whenever you're sitting across from some important person, always picture him sitting there in a suit of long red underwear. That's the way I always operated in business.

—Joseph P. Kennedy

I'll make him an offer he can't refuse.

—Don Corleone, the Godfather

If there were no bad people, there would be no good lawyers.

—Charles Dickens

When you've got them by the wallets, their hearts and minds will follow.

—Verne Naito, Japanese-American consulting magnate

I cannot tell a lie.

—George Washington

Never tell a lie...unless lying is one of your strong points.

—George Washington Plunkitt, former boss of Tammany Hall in New York

Price: Value, plus a reasonable sum for the wear and tear of conscience in demanding it.

—Ambrose Bierce

Buy sheep, sell deer.

—Ancient Babylonian business proverb

A verbal contract isn't worth the paper it's printed on.

—Sam Goldwyn, founder of MGM

Never say you know a man until you have divided an inheritance with him.

—John Lavater

There are some men who, in a fifty-fifty proposition, insist on getting the hyphen too.
—Lawrence J. Peter

If you don't agree with me, it means you haven't been listening.
—Sam Markewich

Final offer: something a veteran negotiator makes just prior to making concessions.
—Jim Fisk and Robert Barron

7
Work

Work is the price you pay for money.

—Anonymous

If a man will not work, he shall not eat.

—2 Thessalonians 3:10

If hard work were such a wonderful thing, surely the rich would have kept it all to themselves.
                    —Lane Kirkland, AFL-CIO president

Work spares us from three great evils: boredom, vice and want.
                                            —Voltaire

Work is the only dirty four-letter word in the language.
                                        —Abbie Hoffman

You seem to have no real purpose in life and won't realize at the age of twenty-two that for a man life means work, and hard work if you mean to succeed.
            —Jennie Jerome Churchill to her twenty-three-
                                    year-old son Winston

Choose a job you love, and you will never have to work a day in your life.

—Confucius

There are few ways in which man can be more innocently employed than in getting money.

—Samuel Johnson

Money does make all the difference. If you have two jobs and you're rich, you have diversified interests. If you have two jobs and you're poor, you're moonlighting.

—Anonymous

We are very different from the rest of the world. Our only natural resource is the hard work of our people.

—Japanese executive

The man who builds a factory builds a temple;
the man who works there worships there.
                                    —Calvin Coolidge

Each morning sees some task begun,
Each evening sees its close.
Something attempted, something done,
Has earned a night's repose.
                        —Henry Wadsworth Longfellow

Work expands so as to fill the time available for
its completion.
                        —C. Northcote Parkinson, creator of
                                        Parkinson's Law

Work is more fun than fun.
                                    —Noël Coward

By working faithfully eight hours a day, you may eventually get to be a boss and work twelve hours a day.

—Robert Frost

God gives the nuts, but He does not crack them.

—Proverb

If my doctor told me I had only six months to live, I wouldn't brood. I'd type a little faster.

—Isaac Asimov

Opportunities are usually disguised as hard work, so most people don't recognize them.

—Ann Landers

8

The Dismal Science

Man does not live by GNP alone.
—Paul Samuelson, Nobel Prize–winning
economist

Economics is a subject that does not greatly respect one's wishes.
—Nikita Khruschev

There's no such thing as a free lunch.
                    —Milton Friedman, Nobel Prize–winning
                                                economist

Family solvency is not a felony, but many economists consider it vaguely unpatriotic.
                                        —Russell Baker

In all recorded history there has not been one
economist who had to worry about where the
next meal came from.
                    —Peter Drucker, dean of American business
                                            commentators

A cynic is someone who knows the cost of everything and the value of nothing.
                                        —Oscar Wilde

There are three kinds of lies: lies, damned lies, and statistics.

—Anonymous

Economic forecasting houses like Data Resources and Chase Econometrics have successfully predicted fourteen of the last five recessions.

—David Fehr, former professor of finance,
Harvard Business School

The inherent vice of capitalism is the unequal sharing of blessings; the inherent vice of socialism is the equal sharing of miseries.

—Winston Churchill

If all the economists in the world were laid end to end, it would probably be a good thing.

—Anonymous

We've been creeping closer to socialism, a system that someone once said works only in heaven, where it isn't needed, and in hell, where they've already got it.

—Ronald Reagan

9
The Game

The object of the game is to make money, hopefully a lot of it.

—"Adam Smith"

Business is a game, the greatest game in the world if you know how to play it.
—Thomas J. Watson, former C.E.O. of IBM

I had a better year than he did.
—Babe Ruth, circa 1929, when asked how he
felt about signing a contract that would bring
him a higher income than President Herbert
Hoover

Most corporate executives have no idea what it
means to earn a buck or make a payroll. They
never see cash coming in. They are playing Monopoly.
—Robert E. Levinson, former vice president of
American Standard Company

Money is just something to make bookkeeping
convenient.
—H. L. Hunt, Texas oil billionaire

Money never meant anything to us. It was just
sort of how we kept score.
—Nelson Bunker Hunt (H. L.'s son)

The only way to keep score in business is to add up how much money you make.
—Harry Helmsley, New York real estate developer and husband of Queen Leona, president of Harley Hotels

The happiest time in any man's life is when he is in red-hot pursuit of a dollar with a reasonable prospect of overtaking it.
—Josh Billings

When you win, nothing hurts.
—Joe Namath

After a certain point, money is meaningless. It ceases to be the goal. The game is what counts.
—Aristotle Onassis

For when the One Great Scorer comes
To write against your name,
He marks—not that you won or lost—
But how you played the game.

—Grantland Rice

10
Bad Advice

A businessman who reads *Business Week* is lost to fame. One who reads Proust is marked for greatness.

—John Kenneth Galbraith

Neither a borrower nor a lender be;
For loan oft loses both itself and friend
And borrowing dulls the edge of husbandry.

—Shakespeare

If it ain't broke, don't fix it—unless you are a consultant.

—Winton G. Rossiter

Pioneering don't pay.

—Andrew Carnegie

No man ever yet became great by imitation.

—Samuel Johnson

Workers of the world, unite!

—Karl Marx

Slow and steady wins the race.
—From "The Tortoise and the Hare," by Aesop

Early to bed and early to rise
Makes a man healthy, wealthy and wise.
                                        —Benjamin Franklin

Early to rise and early to bed
Makes a male healthy, wealthy and dead.
                                        —James Thurber

11

Competition

Competition brings out the best in products and the worst in people.
—David Sarnoff, longtime C.E.O. of RCA

America is the land of opportunity if you're a businessman in Japan.
—Lawrence J. Peter, author of
The Peter Principle

The meek shall inherit the world, but they'll never increase market share.
                    —William G. McGowan, chairman of
                              MCI Communications

Nobody talks more of free enterprise and competition and of the best man winning than the man who inherited his father's store or farm.
                    —C. Wright Mills, sociologist and author of
                                        The Power Elite

Even if you're on the right track, you'll get run over if you just sit there.

                                        —Will Rogers

Whatever is not nailed down is mine. Whatever I can pry loose is not nailed down.
                    —Colis P. Huntington, magnate who helped
                              build the transcontinental railroad

Don't get mad, get even.

—Joseph P. Kennedy

You have undertaken to cheat me. I will not sue you, for the law takes too long. I will ruin you.

—Cornelius Vanderbilt

The biggest things are always the easiest to do because there is no competition.

—William Van Horne

It is only when you are pursued that you become swift.

—Kahlil Gibran

I don't meet competition. I crush it.

—Charles Revson

12
Taxes

And it came to pass in those days, that there went out a decree from Caesar Augustus, that all the world should be taxed.

—St. Luke

Nothing is more inevitable than death and taxes.

—Benjamin Franklin

Of life's two certainties, taxes are the only one for which you can get an automatic extension.

—Jim Fisk and Robert Barron

To tax and to please, no more than to love and to be wise, is not given to men.

—Edmund Burke

IRS = Infernal Revenue Service.

—Anonymous

The income tax has made more liars out of the American people than golf has.

—William Rogers

The taxpayer—that's someone who works for the federal government but doesn't have to take a civil service examination.

—Ronald Reagan

The Good Lord giveth
And Uncle Sam taketh away.

—A Country and Western song

Employees make the best dates. You don't have to pick them up and they're always tax deductible.

—Andy Warhol

13
Pencil Pushers

If I can't take my coffee break, something within me dies.
—From *How to Succeed in Business Without Really Trying*

In a hierarchy, every employee tends to rise to the level of his own incompetence.
—Lawrence J. Peter, author of *The Peter Principle*

Committee: a group that keeps minutes but squanders hours.

—Anonymous

In business, there are four kinds of bees: queen bee, worker bee, drone, and consultant bee.

—Paraphrase of a *New Yorker* cartoon

File cabinet: a four-drawer, manually activated trash compactor.

—Jim Fisk and Robert Barron

Some are born great, some achieve greatness, and some have greatness thrust upon them.

—Shakespeare

Some men are born great, some achieve greatness, and others just keep still.

—Kin Hubbard

14
Women in Business

There are really not many jobs that actually require a penis or vagina, and all other occupations should be open to everyone.

—Gloria Steinem

I object when someone makes overmuch of men's work versus women's work, for I think it is the excellence of the results which counts.

—Margaret Bourke-White, noted photographer

Men seldom make passes
At girls who wear glasses.

—Dorothy Parker

Men seldom make passes
At a girl who surpasses.

—Franklin P. Jones

The best man for the job is a woman.

—Bumper sticker

Back of every achievement is a proud wife and a
surprised mother-in-law.

—Brooks Hays

To be successful, a woman has to be better at her
job than a man.

—Golda Meir

A girl should not expect special privileges because of her sex . . . she must learn to compete . . . not as a woman but as a human being.

—Betty Friedan

I can't type. I can't file. I can't even answer the phone.

—Elizabeth Ray, former secretary to
Congressman Wayne Hayes

If you want something done, give it to a busy man. . . . and he'll have his secretary do it.

—Anonymous

Dear, never forget one little point. It's my business. You just work here.

—Elizabeth Arden, speaking to her husband

15
Corporations

Corporation: an ingenious device for obtaining individual profit without individual responsibility.

—Ambrose Bierce

What's good for General Motors is good for the country.

—Charles E. Wilson, former president of General Motors

They make money the old-fashioned way: they earn it.

> —Advertisement for Smith Barney

We at Chrysler borrow money the old-fashioned way. We pay it back.
> —Lee Iacocca, C.E.O. of Chrysler, when the company made its first repayment of debt backed by U. S. federal loan guarantees

Dividends: Hush money to shareholders.

> —Jim Fisk and Robert Barron

Litigation is the basic legal right which guarantees every corporation its decade in court.

> —David Porter

Going to work for a large company is like getting on a train. Are you going sixty miles an hour, or is the train going sixty miles an hour and you're just sitting still?

—John Paul Getty

16
Profit

The worst crime against the working people is a
company which fails to make a profit.
—Samuel Gompers, founder of International
Workers of the World

Happiness is a positive cash flow.
—Fred Adler, a leading American
venture capitalist

Commerce is mean if it be inconsiderable; but if it be great and abundant . . . it is an enjoyment not much to be censored.

—Cicero

The mechanics of running a business are really not very complicated when you get down to essentials. You have to make some stuff and sell it to somebody for more than it cost you. That's about all there is to it, except for a few million details.

—John L. McCaffrey, former president of International Harvester

The profit motive is not a noble motive. It is not a gallant motive. It is not artistic. It is not dignified. And yet it seems useful.

—Henry Luce

Growth is essential to the good health of an enterprise.

—Alfred P. Sloan, former president of
General Motors

Profitability is the sovereign criterion of the enterprise.

—Peter Drucker

Earnings, except when coercion is present, are essentially rewards for providing the public with what it wants and will willingly pay for with its hard-earned dollars.

—Ernest Henderson, "Mr. Sheraton"

Money in itself doesn't interest me. But you must make money to go on building the business.

—Rupert Murdoch

17

Shady Business

All professions are conspiracies against the laity.
—George Bernard Shaw

Organized crime in America takes in over forty billion dollars a year. This is quite a profitable sum, especially when one considers that the Mafia spends very little for office supplies.
—Woody Allen

Laws are like cobwebs, which may catch small flies but let wasps and hornets break through.
                                    —Jonathan Swift

There's nothing wrong with our business. Lawsuits are the problem.
    —John A. McKinney, chairman of the Manville Corporation, the asbestos producer who filed for bankruptcy in 1983

That's where the money is.
    —Willie Sutton, when asked by a reporter why he robbed banks

Properly organized, even crime pays.
                        —Jim Fisk and Robert Barron

18
Capitalism

The chief business of the American people is business.

—Calvin Coolidge

I've been what's called a capitalist. Some have called me "dirty capitalist"—but I've merely used the imagination and common sense that kind Providence gave me—it made me wealthy—powerful—hated by some—admired by others.

—Daddy Warbucks

Good business is the best art.

—Andy Warhol

There is a serious tendency towards capitalism among the well-to-do peasants.

—Mao Tse-tung

My mistake was buying stock in the company. Now I worry about the lousy work I'm turning out.

—Marvin Townsend

Capital as such is not evil; it is its wrong use that is evil.

—Mahatma Gandhi

Show me a capitalist and I'll show you a blood-sucker.

—Malcolm X

19
Winners

Winning isn't everything—it's the only thing.

—Vince Lombardi

Appearances count; get a sun lamp...maintain an elegant address even if you live in the attic; patronize posh watering holes even if you have to nurse your drink. Never niggle when you're short of cash.

—Aristotle Onassis

There is always room at the top.
                        —Daniel Webster

It feels very, very good and I recommend it to each of you at some point in your lives.
            —Lawrence J. Farley, on becoming C.E.O. of
                            Black and Decker

It's just such a kick. I can't believe they're paying me to do this.
                —George L. Ball, former president of E.F.
            Hutton, commenting on his new position as
                        C.E.O. of Prudential-Bache

When it's raining porridge, you'll always find John's bowl right side up.
            —Lucy Rockefeller, describing her brother
                            John D. as a child

Modesty is a vastly overrated virtue.
—John Kenneth Galbraith

It takes a tough man to make a tender chicken.
—Frank Perdue

I don't have a movie star's ego or an announcer's ego. I have a job. I'm working steady.
—Tom Carvel, founder of the ice cream chain

Back in the old days when I first started, all my buddies would go out drinking and partying while I worked. Now they're working and I'm the one having fun.
—Ron Rice, president of Tanning Research Laboratories

Living well is the best revenge.

—Anonymous

The harder you work the luckier you get.

—Gary Player, golfer

I have just received the following telegram from my generous daddy. It says, "Dear Jack: don't buy a single vote more than is necessary. I'll be damned if I'm going to pay for a landslide."

—John F. Kennedy

20
Losers

The fault, dear Brutus, is not in our stars,
But in ourselves, that we are underlings.

—Shakespeare

He who hesitates is last.

—Mae West

I have my name on the side of the plane. It has got
to do well.
     —Freddie Laker, president of the now-defunct
                                              Laker Airways

Let us be thankful for the fools. But for them the
rest of us could not succeed.
                                              —Mark Twain

Make no small plans: they lack the power to move
men's souls.
     —Cort Randall, president of National Student
Marketing Corporation prior to its bankruptcy

Show me a good loser and I'll show you a loser.
                                              —Jimmy Carter

21
Business Ethics

Business: the art of extracting money from another man's pocket without resorting to violence.
— Max Amsterdam

The closest to perfection a person ever comes is
when he fills out a job application form.
— Stanley J. Randall

It seemed to me, and still does, that the system of American business often produces wrong, immoral and irresponsible decisions, even though the personal morality of the people running the business is often above reproach.
—John Z. DeLorean, speaking about why he left General Motors to form his own "ethical" automobile company

She's the kind of girl who climbed the ladder of success, wrong by wrong.
—Mae West

I don't know as I want a lawyer to tell me what I cannot do. I hire him to tell me how to do what I want to do.
—J. P. Morgan

One who thinks that money can do everything is likely to do anything for money.
—Hasidic saying

The public be damned.

—William Henry Vanderbilt

Virtue has never been as respectable as money.

—Mark Twain

Mere money-making cannot be regarded as the legitimate end . . . since with the conduct of business human happiness or misery is inextricably interwoven.

—Louis Brandeis, former justice of the U. S. Supreme Court

Virtue is not given by money, but from virtue comes money.

—Plato

Principle, *n.* A thing which too many people confound with interest.

—Ambrose Bierce

The bottom line is in heaven.
—Edwin H. Land, founder and inventor of
Polaroid

22
Entrepreneurs

Entrepreneur: a high-rolling risk-taker who would rather be a spectacular failure than a dismal success.

—Jim Fisk and Robert Barron

I always view problems as opportunities in work clothes.

—Henry Kaiser

Great spirits have always found violent opposition from mediocrities.

—Albert Einstein

Don't be afraid to take a big step if one is indicated. You can't cross a chasm in two small jumps.

—David Lloyd George, former prime minister of England

A journey of a thousand leagues begins with a single step.

—Lao-tzu

I was sixty-six years old. I still had to make a living. I looked at my social security check of 105 dollars and decided to use that to try to franchise my chicken recipe. Folks had always liked my chicken.

—Colonel Harland Sanders

Everything has been thought of before, but the problem is to think of it again.

—Goethe

Capital formation is shifting from the entrepreneur who invests in the future to the pension trustee who invests in the past.

—Peter Drucker

Only those who dare to fail greatly can ever achieve greatly.

—Robert F. Kennedy

No guts, no glory.
—Graffito found in a men's washroom, Stanford Business School

It's just as sure a recipe for failure to have the right idea fifty years too soon as five years too late.

—J. R. Platt

You look at any giant corporation, and I mean the biggies, and they all started with a guy with an idea, doing it well.

—Irvine Robbins, founder of Baskin-Robbins

When you want *really* big money, you usually find yourself talking to someone who didn't go to Eton.

—An English banker

They are ill discoverers that think there is no land when they can see nothing but sea.

—Samuel Johnson

Creative thought requires an act of faith.

—George Gilder

To believe your own thought, to believe that
what is true for you is true for all men—that is
genius.

—Ralph Waldo Emerson

23
Inflation

A nickel goes a long way now. You can carry it around for days without finding a thing it will buy.

—Anonymous

When future historians look back on our way of curing inflation, they'll probably compare it to bloodletting in the Middle Ages.

—Lee Iacocca, C.E.O. of Chrysler

A million dollars is not what it used to be.
                              —Howard Hughes, 1937

A billion dollars isn't what it used to be.
                              —Nelson Bunker Hunt

When I first started working I used to dream of the day when I might be earning the salary I'm starving on now.
                              —Anonymous

A dollar saved today is seventy-five cents earned tomorrow.
                    —James Reston, syndicated columnist

The cost of living has gone up another dollar a quart.
                              —W. C. Fields

24
A Search for Excellence

Think.

—Motto of IBM

Training is everything. The peach was once a bitter almond; cauliflower is nothing but cabbage with a college education.

—Mark Twain

The difference between failure and success is doing a thing nearly right and doing a thing exactly right.

—Edward Simmons

He who resolves never to ransack any mind but his own will be soon reduced, from mere barrenness, to the poorest of all imitations: he will be obliged to imitate himself.

—Sir Joshua Reynolds to the students of the Royal Academy of Arts

Few great men could pass Personnel.
—Paul Goodman, author of *Growing Up Absurd*

If all else fails, immortality can always be assured by spectacular error.
—John Kenneth Galbraith, an economist whose immortality is assured

Good is not good where better is expected.
—Thomas Fuller

We have to earn our wings *every* day.
—Frank Borman, former astronaut and president
of Eastern Airlines

Nothing great will ever be achieved without great men, and men are great only if they are determined to be so.
—Charles de Gaulle

25
The Haves

There are only two nations in the world: the haves and the have-nots.

—Cervantes

Let me tell you about the very rich. They are different from you and me.

—F. Scott Fitzgerald

Let me tell you about the very rich. They have checks appeal.

—Thomas Nathaniel Kempner

I'd like to be rich enough so I could throw soap away after the letters are worn off.

—Andy Rooney

That's what God would have done if he had money.

—George S. Kaufman, on first viewing his
partner Moss Hart's remodeled estate

The rich may not live longer, but it certainly seems so to their poor relations.

—Anonymous

In some ways, a millionaire just can't win. If he spends too freely, he is criticized for being extravagant and ostentatious. If, on the other hand, he lives quietly and thriftily, the same people who would have criticized him for being profligate will call him a miser.

—John Paul Getty

Inherited wealth is a real handicap to happiness. It is as certain a death to ambition as cocaine is to morality.

—William K. Vanderbilt

Gentility is what is left over from rich ancestors after the money is gone.

—John Ciardi

Philanthropist. Noun. A rich (and usually bald) old gentleman who has trained himself to grin while his conscience is picking his pocket.

—Ambrose Bierce

If you want to be equal with me, you can get your own Rolls Royce, your own house, and your own million dollars.

—Muhammed Ali

To suppose, as we all suppose, that we could be rich and not behave as the rich behave is like supposing that we could drink all day and stay sober.

—L. P. Smith

If you have to ask how much it costs, you can't afford it.
—J. P. Morgan, Jr., to an observer who inquired how much it cost annually to operate his yacht

The wealthy man is the man who *is* much, not the one who has much.

—Karl Marx

I live by the Golden Rule: he who has the gold makes the rules.

—Anonymous

I've had an exciting life. I married for love and got a little money along with it.

—Rose Kennedy

Ah! But you never had a rich father.
    —Nicky Hilton to his father Conrad, after the latter complained, "I never paid that much for a pair of shoes in all my life."

I'm opposed to millionaires, but it would be dangerous to offer me the position.

—Mark Twain

Wealth: any income that is at least a hundred dollars more a year than the income of one's wife's sister's husband.

—H. L. Mencken

Wealthy people miss one of life's greatest thrills—paying that last installment.

—Anonymous

The rich are dull and they drink too much.

—Ernest Hemingway

26
The Have-Nots

Dear God, I realize it's no disgrace to be poor, but it's no great honor either.

—From *Fiddler on the Roof*

It's easy to be independent when you've got money. But to be independent when you haven't got a thing—that's the Lord's test.

—Mahalia Jackson, gospel singer

It's better to be miserable and rich than it is to be miserable and poor.

—Anonymous

Poor and content is rich—and rich enough.

—Shakespeare

There is nothing more demoralizing than a small but adequate income.

—Edmund Wilson

The best things in life are free.

—Anonymous

My chickens eat better than you do.

—Frank Perdue

You don't seem to realize that a poor person who is unhappy is in a better position than a rich person who is unhappy. Because the poor person has hope. He thinks money would help.

—Jean Kerr

In the planning stages of this survey it was hoped that somewhere in the world a nation would be found whose people are poor but happy. We didn't find such a place.

—George Gallup, pollster

God loves the poor. That is why he made so many of them.

—Anonymous

He who is without cash in pocket might as well be buried in a rice tub with his mouth sewed up.

—Chinese proverb

27
Money

Men sooner forget the murder of their father than the loss of their patrimony.

—John Gardner

In God we trust—all others pay cash.

—Sign in an Arkansas diner

Money is like an arm or a leg—use it or lose it.
                                        —Henry Ford

Money sometimes makes fools of important persons, but it may also make important persons of
fools.
                                        —Walter Winchell

Young people, nowadays, imagine that money is
everything, and when they grow older they know
it.
                                        —Oscar Wilde

Whether he admits it or not, a man has been
brought up to look at money as a sign of his
virility, a symbol of his power, a bigger phallic
symbol than a Porsche.
                                        —Victoria Billings

The love of money is the root of all evil.

—1 Timothy 6:10

Money. The root of all good.

—Minnesota Fats

Money, it turned out, was exactly like sex: you thought of nothing else if you didn't have it, and thought of other things if you did.

—James Baldwin

Money is the most egalitarian force in society. It confers power on whoever holds it.

—Roger Starr

Money helps a man like reality.

—Anonymous

Money brings everything to you, even your daughters.

> —Honoré de Balzac

Money is like a sixth sense without which you cannot make a complete use of the other five.

> —W. Somerset Maugham

The idea all along was to make a hundred million dollars. Otherwise the struggle wouldn't have been worth it. I have American ideals. I love money.

> —Alice Cooper

Money won't buy happiness, but it will pay the salaries of a large research staff to study the problem.

> —Bill Vaughan

Money can't buy friends, but you can get a better class of enemy.

—Spike Milligan

Money is a terrible master but an excellent servant.

—P. T. Barnum

Money is the seed of money, and the first franc is sometimes more difficult to acquire than the second million.

—Jean Jacques Rousseau

A fool and his money are soon parted.

—English proverb

I've got all the money I'll ever need if I die by four o'clock.

—Henny Youngman

Finance is the study of money and how it violates the rules of mathematics and common sense.
—T. Grandon Gill, former president and C.E.O. of SnCorp Industries

I always start a book for money. If you're married five times you have to.

—Norman Mailer

From birth to age eighteen, a girl needs good parents. From eighteen to thirty-five, she needs good looks. From thirty-five to fifty-five, she needs a good personality. From fifty-five on, she needs good cash.

—Sophie Tucker

When it is a question of money, everybody is of the same religion.

—Voltaire

I don't like money, actually, but it quiets my nerves.

—Joe Louis

I believe a little incompatibility is the spice of life, particularly if he has income and she is pattable.

—Ogden Nash

I should like to live like a poor man, with a great deal of money.

—Pablo Picasso

One of the main things money provides is privacy.

> —A member of the Mellon family who declined to be identified for attribution

The evil that men do lives after them.

> —Shakespeare

The money men make lives after them.

> —Samuel Butler

28
Con Artists

There's a sucker born every minute.

—P. T. Barnum

M.B.A.: acronym for several different but related terms: (1) Master of Business Administration; (2) Master Bull Artist; (3) Master of Blind Ambition.

—Jim Fisk and Robert Barron

It's not the money, it's the principle of the thing.
                                        —Anonymous

It's the money.

                                        —Jack Artenstein

Godliness is in league with riches; it is only to the
moral man that wealth comes.
        —Bishop Lawrence (J. P. Morgan's clergyman)

Money doesn't exist because I don't recognize it.
                                        —Bob Dylan

The mark of the true M.B.A. is that he is often
wrong but seldom in doubt.
            —Robert Buzzell, professor of marketing,
                            Harvard Business School

A broker is a man who runs your fortune into a shoestring.

> —Alexander Woollcott, 1930s humorist

Bankruptcy is a legal proceeding in which you put your money in your pants pocket and give your coat to your creditors.

> —Joey Adams

A consultant is someone who will take your watch off your wrist and tell you what time it is.

> —David Owen

Truman's Law: If you can't convince them, confuse them.

> —Harry S. Truman

29
Government

When business accepts help from government, it can be like going to bed with a hippopotamus. It's warm and nice for a moment, but then your bedmate rolls over and crushes you.

—Donald Rumsfeld

There is no country in the world so efficiently governed as the American Telephone and Telegraph Company.

—Ernest Elmo Calkins

The trouble with government regulation of the market is that it prohibits capitalistic acts between consenting adults.

—Robert Nozick

Corrupt, stupid, grasping functionaries will make at least as big a muddle of socialism as stupid, selfish and acquisitive employers can make of capitalism.

—Walter Lippmann

I now know twenty-eight thousand things that won't work—and they're all on salary.
—Ronald Reagan, after taking office as governor of California, discussing state employees

Blessed are the young, for they shall inherit the national debt.

—Herbert Hoover

30
Investing

Never invest your money in anything that eats or needs repainting.
>   —Billy Rose, millionaire entertainment producer

October. This is one of the peculiarly dangerous months to speculate in stocks. The others are July, January, September, April, November, May, March, June, December, August and February.
>   —Mark Twain

The market will not go up unless it goes up, nor will it go down unless it goes down, and it will stay the same unless it does either.

—"Adam Smith"

Brokee: Someone who buys stock on the advice of a broker.

—Jim Fisk and Robert Barron

Jesus saves, Moses invests.

—Anonymous

Tell your friends who made money on IBM that beating the market may work in practice, but it no longer works in theory.

—Jim Fisk and Robert Barron on the Efficient Market Hypothesis

In Wall Street, the only thing that's hard to explain is next week.

   —Louis Rukeyser, on *Wall Street Week*

Bulls make money and bears make money, but pigs seldom do.

   —Wall Street maxim

Buy low, sell high.

   —Anonymous

Don't try to buy at the bottom and sell at the top. This can't be done—except by liars.

   —Bernard Baruch

Should the market slip five points, remember that's only 2.8 Celcius.

   —Anonymous

I never attempt to make money on the stock market. I buy on the assumption that they could close the market the next day and not reopen it for five years.

—Warren Buffett, C.E.O. of Berkshire Hathaway Corporation and famous stock speculator, reputed to have made more than 400 million dollars in the stock market

Put all your eggs in one basket and—*watch that basket*.

—Andrew Carnegie

The game of professional investment is intolerably boring and overexacting to anyone who is entirely exempt from the gambling instinct; whilst he who has it must pay to this propensity the appropriate toll.

—John Maynard Keynes

Buy old masters. They fetch a much better price
than old mistresses.

—Lord Beaverbrook

Gentlemen prefer bonds.

—Andrew Mellon

31
Experience

Experience: a comb life gives you after you lose your hair.

—Judith Stern

Between twenty-five and thirty-five you're too young to do anything well; after thirty-five you're too old.

—Fritz Kreisler

Experience is what enables you to recognize a mistake when you make it again.

—Earl Wilson

If you could sell your experience for what it cost you, you would have a fortune.

—Herbert Prochnow

A man who is not a liberal at sixteen has no heart. A man who is not a conservative at sixty has no head.

—Benjamin Disraeli

Experience is the name everyone gives to their mistakes.

—Oscar Wilde

32
Hiring, Firing, Retiring

It is all one to me if a man comes from Sing Sing or Harvard. We hire a man, not his history.

—Henry Ford

Don't hire Harvard Business School graduates. This worthy enterprise confesses that it trains its students for only three posts—executive vice president, president, and board chairman.

—Robert Townsend, former president of Avis

Promotion: new title, new salary, new office, same old crap.

—Jim Fisk and Robert Barron

No matter what the job is, it ain't final. You can always quit.

—Peter Drucker

Mr. Morgan buys his partners; I grow my own.

—Andrew Carnegie

Retirement at sixty-five is ridiculous. When I was sixty-five, I still had pimples.

—George Burns

33
The Wheel of Fortune

Chance is the pseudonym God uses when He'd rather not sign His own name.

—Anatole France

An ounce of fortune is worth a pound of forecast.

—Anonymous

Up and down the city road,
In and out the eagle,
That's the way the money goes—
Pop goes the weasel!

—Anonymous

When luck is on your side, you can do without
brains.
        —Giordano Bruno, Italian philosopher and
    scientist who was burned at the stake by the
                         Inquisition in 1600

Life is a misery if you don't get more than you
deserve.
        —Harry Oppenheimer, C.E.O. of De Beers
                         Consolidated Mines

34
Words to the Wise

The meek may inherit the earth, but not its mineral rights.

—John Paul Getty

Buy low, sell high, collect early, and pay late.
—Dick Levin, author and associate dean of the
School of Business Administration, University of
North Carolina

If you have no money, be polite.

—Danish proverb

Of money, wit and virtue, believe one-fourth of what you hear.

—Proverb

Be awful nice to 'em goin' up, because you're gonna meet 'em all comin' down.

—Jimmy Durante

If you pick up a starving dog and make him prosperous, he will not bite you. This is the principal difference between a dog and a man.

—Mark Twain

I have always observed that to succeed in the world one should seem a fool but be wise.

—Charles de Montesquieu

We work on the KISS system. KISS is short for "Keep It Simple, Stupid."

—Ray Kroc

I've always been worried about people who are willing to work for nothing. Sometimes that's all you get from them, nothing.

—Sam Ervin, former U. S. senator

It was a friendship founded on business, which is a good deal better than a business founded on friendship.

—John D. Rockefeller

Only hire people you'd be happy to have in your home and play poker with.

—Dick Kress, president of Norelco

Where large sums of money are concerned, it is advisable to trust nobody.

—Agatha Christie

If at first you don't succeed, try, try again . . . then give up. There's no use being a damn fool about it.

—W. C. Fields

Caveat emptor.

—Anonymous